MW01600530

PERMISSION TO LIVE

PERMISSION TO LIVE

. . .

Six Practical Steps
to Consistently Overcome

. . .

Jason P. Sanderson

TATE PUBLISHING
AND **ENTERPRISES**, LLC

Permission to Live
Copyright © 2012 by Jason P. Sanderson. All rights reserved.

No part of this publication may be reproduced, stored in a retrieval system or transmitted in any way by any means, electronic, mechanical, photocopy, recording or otherwise without the prior permission of the author except as provided by USA copyright law.

The opinions expressed by the author are not necessarily those of Tate Publishing, LLC.

This book is designed to provide accurate and authoritative information with regard to the subject matter covered. This information is given with the understanding that neither the author nor Tate Publishing, LLC is engaged in rendering legal, professional advice. Since the details of your situation are fact dependent, you should additionally seek the services of a competent professional.

Published by Tate Publishing & Enterprises, LLC
127 E. Trade Center Terrace | Mustang, Oklahoma 73064 USA
1.888.361.9473 | www.tatepublishing.com

Tate Publishing is committed to excellence in the publishing industry. The company reflects the philosophy established by the founders, based on Psalm 68:11,
"The Lord gave the word and great was the company of those who published it."

Book design copyright © 2012 by Tate Publishing, LLC. All rights reserved.
Cover design by Shawn Collins
Interior design by Lucia Kroeger Renz

Published in the United States of America

ISBN: 978-1-61862-941-8
1. Religion / General
2. Self-Help / Spiritual
12.06.19

TABLE OF CONTENTS

FOREWORD

In *Permission to Live*, Pastor Jason Sanderson reaches down into our innermost beings and speaks right to the essential core of who we are. Jason addresses issues that are far too often overlooked or ignored because of a fear of change. In a day and age when technology changes as fast as it is created, people unfortunately are changing slower and slower. In his wonderful work, Jason removes every excuse and challenges us to break through the barriers that have kept us from truly being who we were created to be.

In the following pages you hear the heart cry of a man who has admittedly been a prisoner to this war, yet when rescued by the Love of Jesus became an advocate to rescue others. I know Pastor Jason Sanderson very well. He was the best man in my wedding and has been a tremendous influence in my own life both personally and professionally. In my sixteen years of youth ministry I've made it a practice to invite Jason with me in any ministry setting possible. We've been in the jungles of Peru, youth camps, churches, and conferences all over the United States. Having known him his entire life, I know that once he found "permission to live" it has been a life lived on purpose.

His contagious zeal for life permeates these pages as you discover through humor, wisdom, and divine insight that we all long to live a life with a meaning greater than ourselves. His writing style is fresh and unique and his imagery is captivating while leaving you wanting more. For years people have grown up in families and churches that have told them to sit still and be quiet. This has caused generations to live in bondage and captivity for people have become performers of basic functions rather than proclaimers of liberty. People have voluntarily allowed themselves to be imprisoned and Jason tackles it head-on with a practical and passionate plea.

His heart cry dares you to dream and double-dares you to reach for the stars for once you touch them you too will shine with the brilliance of an Almighty Creator. Whether you are in middle-management, you work in a factory, or are a student, this book is a must read. For those who are just starting out, memorize these pages. For those who've been burned out, let these pages breathe new life. No matter what season we find ourselves at in our lives we can all fall into the lethargic trap of routine. While being intentional and having schedules are important, sometimes we need a fresh perspective to take us from simply being alive to thrive. Greatness is never achieved by those sitting on the sidelines of life.

Jason invites you to, not only get into the game, but to make the greatest contribution you didn't even know you could make. Begin your journey now and discover that you have permission to proclaim, pray, praise, position, play, and practice!

—Pastor Billy Sanderson, Jr.

INTRODUCTION

When I first thought of *Permission to Live,* I was considering all the people out there just waiting to live their lives. These people, including you and me, were, are, or at one time sought out permission of all things. Maybe it was/is permission from themselves? The reason I say this with conviction is that I was recently one of these people. I followed my heart to the places I thought I was "supposed" to go, and I was still left with a sense of emptiness. Where did the emptiness come from, and if I'm following Jesus, why and how could I possibly feel this way?

At our church, we once had the privilege of hosting a conference with guest speaker Dr. John Stanko. Dr. John is best known for his purpose message and, boy, did he get through to me—so much so that I decided to hire out his services in the area of "purpose coaching." Here I stood, a worship pastor of a local church just biding my time, fulfilling due diligence and all the while no closer, or at least feeling closer, to what I thought God had for me.

No one wants to be told what to do, but most everyone is looking for permission to do it—whether they know it or not. Permission to feel significant, permission to make an impact on this world, and permission to do something greater than you or me, even when the Christian world would try to tell you that you're not! There seems to be no greater sense of discouragement when you have a dream and you don't even feel as though those closest to you will encourage you. Something's not quite right when this is the case, so that's why understanding permission and applying it is so important.

A couple years ago, I was sitting in the passenger seat of my Yukon XL, and I only put the "XL" in there because it sounds sweeter. My wife was driving us back from Dallas. Guess what we had just got finished doing? I'll give you a minute…Conjure up something radical, get my email, or facebook me, and tell me what you thought it was before you continue reading. I'm literally going to leave the rest of this page blank just so you have to turn it to find out. I want you to guess!

I had just auditioned for America's Got Talent, a TV show that has three celebrity judges determining who has talent and who doesn't. How crazy is that? It was quite the experience. Just so you don't wonder, no, I didn't make it through, but it sure was fun. I loved just getting in front of three judges who obviously didn't know anything because they didn't pick me, but still having the opportunity to pour out what God gave me into three complete strangers. It was great, even if they didn't have taste. Here's the point: I gave myself permission to succeed or fail. I proclaimed to the world in my own way that Jason P. Sanderson is on his way to the top. I'm not allowing people, places, or things to dictate where the top is or how I'm supposed to get there— except Jesus. Isn't that the point, anyway? But we wrestle with this constantly.

This is what's so amazing about the permission concept. At this juncture, I feel the need to clarify one thing. I am not and will never advocate permission to go against the Word of God. These next chapters are not promoting the free will movement to do whatever makes you happy. There are and will be many times that God asks us to wait on Him, and to, as the Bible puts it in James 1:4, "let patience have her perfect work." I am, however, saying that we get so bogged down with fear and are too focused on being in the perfect will of God that we never even get in His will. We dance around our dreams, hoping that someone will make it happen all while we never fulfill what God himself placed in us for the here and now. We have to remove the blinders of specificity in what ways we can be used by God. We need to open the creativeness that was interwoven into the very fibers of our beings before the world was made. Job 10:8 tells us that his hands formed us into an intricate unity. What a powerful description! We have to grasp the magnitude of how amazing God is in our lives and that he knows us better than we do. So let's get specific and actually learn six practical ways we can apply permission.

PERMISSION TO PROCLAIM

In a soft and mundane voice, the phone call began, "Hey, honey, I think we need to get divorced. I'm not good for you or the kids. You don't know what kind of man I am."

Her response, "What are you talking about? You're not making any sense!"

Again his tone was cautious and calm as he said, "I wish I could explain more, but I can't." You could hear the hurt, remorse, guilt and shame in his voice. She was devastated, stunned, and overwhelmed. To say she was caught off guard would be a drastic understatement. With three kids under the age of seven, how her mind could think about what she's going to do, where she's going to go, and how her kids were ever going to be normal with this as a part of their legacy was just too much to process.

He was working and couldn't give her more time to sift through the rubble of the explosion that he just set off. Confused and desperate, she picked up the phone and called their pastor. In a baffled mindset, she offered up a plea for help.

The man ignored the first call from their pastor, ironically thanking God for caller ID. The second call wasn't as easy to ignore, but, nonetheless, he found the strength. When the third call didn't happen, he was almost offended. Was it that easy for his pastor to give up on him? After taking a moment to collect the confusion and aftermath of the situation he just set in motion, he painstakingly and reluctantly called his pastor. "Hey, Pastor, what's going on?" He was not sure whether he was trying to convince himself or the pastor that he was okay.

"I'm doing fine. What's going on with you?" And then, with compassion and a sense of commanding an answer, the pastor continued, "I just got off the phone with your wife."

Crap! wasn't the only thought that came to his mind, but it sure was resounding.

With purpose and a whole lot of clarity, the pastor proclaimed, "You and I are meeting tonight."

It's hard to believe that just four months after that phone call, I was hired on as the full-time worship/staff pastor for our church! I'm sure that you have many questions. "What was that pastor thinking hiring him?" He wasn't thinking, and we are still praying for his salvation! In all seriousness, my pastor showed me who Jesus looked like in that moment, gave me tools, and believed in me.

What a way to kick off your career in ministry, huh?

We are going to get into the rest of this story through-out the book as I show you the steps I took. As I watched myself, my marriage, and my ministry blossom beyond what I ever could've imagined on that gut-wrenching October night, I sat down with my pastor.

. . .

But for this purpose I have raised you up, to show you my power, so that my name may be proclaimed in all the earth.

Exodus 9:16 (ESV)

Here we see God speaking to Pharaoh about the main purpose of all life—to see God's name proclaimed in *all* the earth. This is why we are here on this earth—to pro-claim his name and show people that no matter the depths of the crisis you are facing, our God is able, and he alone deserves the glory. God desires to raise you up and to show his mighty power, that you would proclaim his name. Maybe you have an incredible story of redemption. Please, I beg you, in every way possible, proclaim his glory for your victory. Maybe you're in the beginning or middle of your redemption process. You need to start proclaiming who God is in your life. His worthiness far extends past any and all circumstances we are currently facing. I've heard it said on many different occasions, and the saying goes like this: "When you're going through hell, don't stop!"

The phrase "don't stop" is a recurring theme throughout this book, and I hope that it becomes a mantra in your life.

The main reason I chose to start off with proclaiming, first and foremost, is that's what Jesus did. When Jesus was tempted in Matthew 4, what did he do? He proclaimed the Word of God. He didn't fall on his knees and beg God to get him out of the situation or pray incessantly that if God helped him past this trial he would serve God forever. Isn't that what we as Christians do, though? Let me answer for you, just in case you forgot, what you normally tend to do. Does this next sentence sound familiar? "Oh, God, infinite Father of time and space, Almighty Maker of all things good, Counselor to the just, have Your way as long as it doesn't hurt too badly and as long as you don't ask too much of me." We get so caught up in the "me" and "my" that we neglect the power of the Word of God and proclaiming it over our lives.

I had to start speaking the Word of God over my life, and so do you—over your marriage and children, over your job and finances, and over every area of your life. The enemy was incessantly reminding me of the pain I had caused and what a failure of a husband and father I had turned out to be. Even I reminded myself of the screw up I'd become. But I didn't stay there. I had to grab hold of and cling to his Word with every ounce of strength I had. You will have to do the same. Nothing that is worth anything in this life is easy to come by. You may say salvation was easy. That depends on who you're asking. I'll bet Jesus would argue over that. Let's look to Jesus to see how he proclaimed the Word of God: He did not look forward to the crucifixion. He prayed that this cup would pass from him. But he submitted himself to the Father and declared, "Nevertheless, not my will but yours be done" (Luke 22:42).

Because of my own failures, I was stuck and trying to place blame on others, especially my wife. You know how it goes: we typically will try to find faults in others to somehow make our own faults not seem so repulsive. This, in turn, pushes away the very people we want and, more importantly, need to help us. I've counseled with a lot of people and what I've found is that when a person is guilty of something, a common practice is for that person to accuse others, usually those they're closest to, of the wrong he or she has done. For example, a person who has cheated on his or her spouse will turn around and begin accusing the spouse of cheating when there has been no evidence whatsoever to substantiate that claim. The same would go for someone who begins lying to cover up whatever he feels guilty about.

I know that this is where I found myself, and the only way to overcome it was to speak the truth. Most people wrongly assume that the truth is where someone is at any given point. Let's say a person is cheating, so someone would say the truth is that person is a cheater. I say they're wrong. The momentary fact is that person is a cheater, but the truth has to come from the Word of God. The Word of God is the only truth that we should ever live our lives by. The truth over that person is that even though he was bound, he can be set free! What an incredible difference it makes in our lives when we begin to see others through what the Word of God says about them and not what the current facts say. What about you? What have you believed about yourself that has been a fact, but is not the truth?

You see, I had to begin to tell my circumstance what it was going to become. My wife was not always my best friend, and as long as I told myself she wasn't, that's exactly what I was going to get. I began telling her, the kids, and anyone else who would listen that she was my best friend and you know what? That's exactly what she has become. But I didn't stop there. I continue to say it. Maybe your situation is the same as mine, or maybe you're dealing with depression, anger, lust, jealous—you name it. God designed the world in such a way that when our words line up with the Word, impossible things become possible. What are you going to start speaking over your life?

The Bible says that God "calls into existence the things that do not exist" (Romans 4:17, ESV). In other words, we can take after his example and speak those things that "be not as though they were." He's saying, "Speak it into existence because I, God, set it up that way!" God spoke the world into existence. He didn't pray until he fell asleep, or cry a river, or agonize; He spoke! You see, it's not enough to just say it in your head like so many Christians do. The world needs to hear (Romans 10:17) the voice of God in and through you. So let it be heard. Note that this doesn't mean you can take advantage of this by being irresponsible. For instance, speaking a car into your life when you're not even taking care of the one you have now. God can and does move despite us, but I also believe He expects us to be good stewards of what He's all ready blessed us with.

I want to give you permission to proclaim to yourself how great you are. More importantly, I want you to give yourself permission to say it. I want you to say it right now: I am great! Some of you are saying it but not believing it. Say it again. I am great! Not because of you but because you're made in God's image (Genesis 1:27). One more time: I am great! If we're ever to influence the hearts of those that need him, we need to think and act differently. People want to follow greatness, not cockiness or haughtiness—greatness. But more times than not, they need to see it in you first so they will take hold of the truth that is God.

When you're in the middle of your mess it's hard to believe that any part of you is great. It's very difficult to believe that God cares or even has a plan to use all of your junk, but I assure you he does. This is where the mindset has to change. It's not about you, and it's all about you. Contradictory, huh? No, your worth and justification come through Jesus. But Jesus is not going to open your mouth, use you like a ventriloquist, and speak it for you. At times, I would sure appreciate it if Jesus would do this, but he's not going to. We have to put some work behind our faith (James 2:17). I do, however, want to warn against a fake form of faith.

Many times I've witnessed Christians operate in a false humility that makes me want to vomit. Sorry for being graphic, but I want to properly articulate my disdain. "Oh, it's not me, it's God in me." We've got the Christian vernacular down to an art. We imitate what we hear in such a robotic way that we disregard the very uniqueness of who God made us. Be yourself; I give you permission. Most importantly, God gives you permission. That's not to say you're to go dancing around naked saying, "Jason and God told me to be 'myself'!" All I'm saying is stop imitating and start being the image of you that *no one* else can or will ever be. Got it? Good. Now let's move on.

Let's take some steps toward bringing about this much needed freedom.

Proclaim the Word of God. Nothing is as life changing or life giving as the living Word of God.

> **Nothing is as life changing or life giving as the living Word of God.**
> •

You will need this to be the foundation for all other steps and processes. Give yourself permission to recite just one scripture a day. Note to self: Do not get caught up in the lie that you *have* to know the verse and chapter. Does it help to know the verse and chapter? Absolutely, but it is not the only way. Let me prove it to you. What better example than Jesus. Jesus did not combat the enemy with references. You know why? Because there were no references back then. The Holy Spirit did not inspire a reference—man did. I'm very grateful for references, though. There is importance in knowing where to turn to in the Bible and pointing people to them, but as you start out, don't be defeated by this mentality.

Here's what Jesus's reference was: "It is written…"

For you and me, we just need to start somewhere and don't stop—whatever you do, *don't stop*!

I'm reminded of a story from my childhood. There was woman who I knew, and her name was Mrs. Roland. I can't think of her first name. Mrs. Roland, though, was one incredible woman. She invested ten dollars into my life, and it changed me forever. You might say, "Ten dollars? What's so big about ten dollars?" Well, that's the price it took for her to get me to recite Psalm 121 from memory to her, which states:

> [1] I will lift up my eyes to the mountains; from where shall my help come?

[2] My help comes from the Lord, Who made heaven and earth.

[3] He will not allow your foot to slip; He who keeps you will not slumber.

[4] Behold, He who keeps Israel will neither slumber nor sleep.

[5] The Lord is your keeper; The Lord is your shade on your right hand.

[6] The sun will not smite you by day, nor the moon by night.

[7] The Lord will protect you from all evil; He will keep your soul.

[8] The Lord will guard your going out and your coming in from this time forth and forever.

Psalm 121:1-8 (NASU)

I practiced this scripture hardcore, and I was dedicated. I wanted that ten dollars, and nothing was getting in my way. This passage of scripture has stuck with me my entire life. You see, she was onto something. She understood the value of the spoken Word of God. Mrs. Roland gave me incentive to read, memorize, and, most importantly, *speak* the Word of God. As it states in verse eight, God has seen to it and has guarded me even from myself. How many of you reading this right now are saying, "Man, oh, man, do

I needing guarding from myself"? Just take a wild guess at who can do this for you.

So what did Jesus do when he was tempted? Surprisingly, when I asked different groups of people this question, I found that they didn't know. Most said that he prayed, and some said that he walked away. We know that he quoted and spoke the Word of God. Yes, Jesus quoted the Word of God. Is it just me, or does that sound weird to you too? Here's the living breathing God, and he's quoting himself. What arrogance! No, *confidence* in what the Word can do.

In this instance you will see that Jesus didn't fall down on his face wailing and pleading with God to deliver him out of the situation.

Hopefully you will agree and allow me to pose this question. What has our conditioned response been to the temptations of the enemy (Satan)? I'll give you some examples. Most people will start to fret and question God asking, "Why do I continue to struggle with this?" and "Where are You, God?" What about the guilt and shame for falling once again when you truly have a heart after God's? If this rings true, trust me that there is great hope, and these steps are the right tools to effectively and consistently overcome.

Here are some other conditioned responses. What about the "seasoned" Christians? Seasoned Christians will employ their 911 hotline of prayer warriors the moment they sneeze. I can just see them now, "Mary Sue…now, you know that I've been struggling with this cold for fifteen years, but this case seems like it's much, much worse, and I'm gonna need to you to implement the breakthrough prayer brigade on my behalf." I'm not negating the power of prayer or the necessity of it. Although prayer is essential, I don't believe it should be our first response. Our first response should be to speak the Word of God over the situation and then pray.

What I am saying is this: follow the very example of the One who created us in his image, in the likeness of him, for the very purpose of imitating every step, word, and thought he set out before us. Declare the Word of God before calling up the prayer brigade. Do what Jesus did: proclaim, "It is written!"

Let's face it, we've tried it our way, it's not working and it doesn't work. We believe that God is big and he can do anything, but we struggle with believing that he can actually do it through us.

Here's what Colossians 3:10 says, "Put on your new nature, and be renewed as you *learn* to know your Creator and become like him."

If we are to walk out our salvation as the Bible so clearly states, then we need to *learn* to know our Creator and become like him. This word *learn* implies that we will never know everything there is to know about God and that we can always become more like him. Once you come to grips with the fact that you can never know it all, there's a freedom and relief from the pressure of needing to have it all together.

Once you come to grips with the fact that you can never know it all, there's a freedom and relief from the pressure of needing to have it all together.

. . . .

Here I am, leading worship for our church, my marriage is falling apart, my life isn't making sense, and I keep trying to solve all the issues *my way*. Even in my limited experience working for the church full time, I've witnessed far too many leaders trying to fake it and make it on their own terms. This breaks my heart because it will never work.

One of my favorite pastors is Brady Boyd, Senior Pastor of New Life Church in Colorado Springs, CO. He said something at a conference I once attended that resonated with the very core of my being. I'm paraphrasing, but he said that he doesn't desire to work with anyone who hasn't been through a major crisis at one time or another. His premise behind this was that if they've never had to overcome some things, how can they know what they'll do in the face of adversity?

Pastor Brady also spoke a word over my life that changed me forever. He doesn't know me, but he has mentored me in so many ways. Praise God! If you ever get your hands on this book, Pastor Brady, give me a call. We'll do lunch.

So let's get back to what is happening in the life of Jesus as it pertains to Colossians 3:10. We've got to realize that

Jesus was showing us something. He was saying, "Learn and imitate Me!" I'm showing you the way...wait, what's that verse? John 14:6. Jesus is speaking to Thomas. Here we find that Jesus says, "I am *the Way* and the Truth and the Life. No one comes to the Father but through Me." We get caught up with the Truth and the Life but neglect to remember he said I am *the Way*. "The Way" means that whatever He did is *the Way* to do the whatever it is you need to do or get done.

Let's complete an exercise together right now! Take in a deep breath...Now let it out and repeat after me: I do not have it all together. One more time. I do not have it all together. Make sure you say this out loud.

Having done this, can't you all ready begin to feel release? Admitting that the stench we smell oftentimes is actually coming from us, and not the people we are judging, is quite freeing. Let's get real and make the most of the time we're allotted down here.

Now that we've established a few things, let's back track and review them before we move on.

You don't have it all together, and it's okay. God still loves you, and so do your friends and family. In fact, most of your friends and family have been waiting for you to realize this. The others may need you to break the mold so they can realize they don't have it all together either.

Jesus gives us the example of *the Way*. Speak the Word of God over your life. Live the way Jesus did.

I am great! Well, you are great, and you need to believe it. God doesn't make anything less.

So, in essence, when you realize that you've got some growing to do and you begin to speak the Word of God over you, then you will understand that God created greatness inside you, and the way to get it out is to proclaim it!

Permission granted.

PERMISSION TO PRAY

That October night in 2006 when I met with my pastor, we began to discuss what was really going on with me. It was a rough moment. Now, I don't consider myself an expert on inner healing, but I've been through numerous programs, and I've studied this topic to great lengths. What I've found to be true is that people can go to therapy for years and read all the self-help books they want with twelve steps to do this or that and still have no success. You can even read this book with its six practical steps, but one real and authentic moment with Jesus is the key. Yes, we still have to walk it out, but if it doesn't start with Jesus, it most likely will fail.

I have watched and witnessed firsthand more people set free with one word from Jesus than the countless appointments people keep with therapists, all the while no closer to true freedom. Something that has become a mantra in my life is this: I can speak a word to you, and it might influence you or even move you to take some action. But one word from God and you're changed, made free, and are no longer a slave to sin! Just one word!

We were sitting in his office, and I was fighting back the sobs (crying like a little girl) of past pain that was holding me hostage. I was telling him that I knew this was years ago, but it was so hard to let go. I had never told my wife, Tisa—what would she think of me? How could God forgive me? How could Tisa forgive me, and how was I going to forgive myself?

As I began to just pour out my past sin (James 5:16) beneath overwhelming sobs, the prison I was captive in for so long came crashing down all around me. It was there in that moment of genuine and authentic prayer that I let the power of what Jesus did on the cross make me free. It was one phrase Jesus spoke to me that changed it all. In what was authentic prayer to Jesus, I was made free.

We all need to know that freedom is a lifestyle and not just a moment. I often tell my children that character is not defined in the big choices we make but in the everyday, little decisions. I hope that your Christian walk is not defined by one prayer but by many prayers that cultivate a relationship with our Savior.

I want to address fake prayer vs. authentic prayer.

In the first chapter, I referred to "conditioned responses" by Christians. These responses are based off of common verbiage heard around religious circles. Or, as the Bible so plainly puts it in Matthew 6:7, "empty phrases."

I was praying with my children one night, and I realized I had heard the prayer coming from my son before.

Now where could I have possibly heard it? Well it was the same one he had been praying every night. That night, however, it bothered me, and I challenged him to actually think about what he was praying. We had become so stuck in routine that even our prayers were repetitive and lacked any type of connection with God. Matthew 6:7 was ringing loud and clear that night. In what was authentic prayer from my son, I could sense and see his demeanor changing from nonchalant to purposeful. Praise Jesus.

I heard a comedian one time talk about prayer. In fact, it was Tim Hawkins, and he was making fun of some of the vernacular we use to pray for one another. This specific example was talking about the phrase "hedge of protection." He made light of the phrase by asking people not to pray a hedge because he believed "shrubbery" isn't going to help him very much. He wanted people to pray for a concrete wall of protection for him. I'm inclined to agree.

Haven't we done this as the church, though? We hear someone pray a prayer, and we steal their phrases because somehow we feel as though their words are on an expressway to the ears of heaven. We don't want to take the time to build our own relationship with Jesus, so we borrow phrases that haven't been birthed out of our own cries to God, out of the prison we've captured ourselves in.

Prayer is not all about the way that you feel. In fact, Christianity is not about the way you feel. Feelings get Christians in so much junk that it's not surprising that so many marriages in the church end in divorce. To those of you who are married or who are planning to someday, your marriage is not entirely about feelings; it's about love—real love, authentic love—the kind that Christ demonstrated on the cross. There's nothing wrong with feelings, but when they control your decisions, the problems begin. I'm sure that Jesus didn't *feel* like dying, but because of his great love, he did, and that has made a world of difference.

King David put it this way, "Bless the Lord oh my soul, and all that is within me, bless His Holy name" (Psalms 103:1, ESV).

The way that I read this text is that we are to command our souls (mind, will, and emotions) to bless His name. It's not a suggestion; it's a command. So why don't we command our souls to love our spouses? Would that ultimately honor God? You bet your ripped jeans it would and does.

Soapbox over, let's move on.

Here's what I believe most people are looking for. They want a prayer by way of a formula to solve all their problems. Let me prove it to you. I'm in no way trying to place a negative spin on the power of praying certain things over your life, but when you look more to the words than the One who created them, you get in trouble. The Prayer of Jabez is a perfect example. Too many people believed that if they just prayed this prayer that God would pop out like a genie and grant them the desires of their sweet, little hearts. I've prayed that prayer many times but only as way to enhance my communication with God, not as a way to get something from Him. I have certainly been guilty of this in the past, though.

Take this next sentence and apply it to every part of your life. It's not merely about the method; it's mainly about the motive. Your motive will drive you to find the right method. The same can't be said if we start out seeking a method.

> ## It's not merely about the method; it's mainly about the motive.
> ·

The motive of your heart can, will, and does guide your every action. Again, we find that King David asked God to search his what? *Heart*. David knew that his heart had to be found pure before God in order to serve him in full capacity. Your prayers to God should mainly be about motive—not method. What's your motive when you go before your Maker? Is it a family crisis and all you want him for is to fix it? Has your favorite pet cat come down with a serious illness, and who knows how you'll make it without Sparky in your life? (We all know that cats don't go to heaven—just dogs. Just watch the movie, folks.) That was for Pastor Craig Groeschel, another mentor of mine that I've yet to meet.

I truly believe that Jesus is waiting for us to be real. Let's define what being real means. I'm going to step on a few toes here, but just love me anyway.

You know that emotional or physical affair that you're having or had with someone other than your spouse? All the feelings that stir up inside you, making you feel as though there's something wrong with your marriage—or life, for that matter. Here's where being real comes in. Jesus is waiting for you to talk to him about all that! He's not mad that you're having those feelings; he just doesn't want you to act on them. He wants you to pour out those feelings on him. He can take it. He desires to show you a better way and channel those feelings in the right direction. So where does prayer come in, you say? Prayer is simply what I've just stated—talking to Jesus.

Oh, and you're not off the hook, either, Mr. or Miss "my life doesn't make any sense, and I don't want to live in this depression/pain anymore!" He doesn't want you to live in it anymore, either. He just wants you to be open about it and cry out to him instead of to the drugs, bars, sex, cutting, etc. Basically, just insert your story here

_____

and ask yourself if you've talked to Jesus about everything—not just some of it. Plainly and simply put, prayer is just talking with Jesus and developing a relationship with Him.

I vividly remember standing at the kitchen sink one afternoon doing dishes. I was so frustrated with my life and so mad at God for allowing all the negative things that had happened to me. I was even mad at him for letting me do some of the dumb things I had done. Sounds crazy when I think back on it, but it wasn't crazy to me at the time.

Then all of a sudden, I just started yelling at God. I was screaming. I told him every emotion I was feeling and asked him how he could let all of this happen. I asked him why he didn't protect me and keep me even from myself. I can't tell you that I got all the answers, but he sure did speak to me. He started off with one word: *Finally.* "Finally?" I asked. In the quietness and stillness in my mind, the thoughts that came flooding were, *Finally you've decided to get real and let me know how you really feel.* I was blown away by the peace that swept in my kitchen and the sense that he was there.

So why, if it's so easy, doesn't everyone do it? Because people pray, and when their prayers aren't answered within their timetable, they give up. And in their giving up they never truly develop a relationship with Jesus. They never truly understand what it means to wait on Him and to trust that His ways and plans for our lives are better than our own. Others talk to Jesus and then rely on their feelings as to whether or not their talk was effective. Both are surefire ways to a failed relationship with our Creator. I've often found myself saying to Jesus, "I'm not happy right now, but I trust You more than I trust myself." This is where it gets hard and is why most won't do it. So our job then is to *not* be most people.

Sitting in my pastor's office and crying out to God, I realized that although I had a head knowledge of what I was supposed to do, my heart wasn't in it. I came to know Jesus in such an authentic way that evening.

One of the things that recently hit me as I was talking to a man in our church was that Jesus loved me through the pain I caused. He will love you through the pain that you've caused as well. Even if you haven't caused any pain, he is there waiting to love. His love reached and continues to reach down passing all disappointment, resentment, pain, unforgiveness, any and all things you've gone through or are currently going through. He was still loving me and you even when my back was completely turned! What an amazing God we serve!

So where are you at in this process? Are you struggling to trust that God truly knows better and his ways are higher? Ask yourself these key questions and pour out your response to him. When you come back around to it, each time you talk to God, begin by checking off these next few questions.

1. Is my motive pure, or am I just interested in a method? Do I just want something?

2. In my prayer, am I really going to trust Jesus with the outcome no matter what?

3. Am I only talking to God when I feel like it, or am I pressing in when I don't?

I really didn't want to talk with my pastor that night, but when I pressed in and trusted Jesus with the outcome, it was greater than I could have ever imagined. I got real with Jesus, and you can too. Why don't you take the time right now and get real for a moment? Ask God to reveal areas in your life that are fake. Ask for the boldness to face past pain. It's worth it!

Permission granted to have real prayer.

PERMISSION TO PRAISE

So imagine yourself as the senior pastor of a church, maybe you are, and your worship pastor/leader comes to you, their life falling apart, and confesses a story to you that you weren't expecting. What would you have done? Well, per my pastor's confession, he was a little beside himself as for what to do. To God's glory, he turned the matter over to Jesus.

I just knew that my past sin would mean that I was going to be asked to step down for a season. Through it all I was learning that my past was who I was and not who I am today. Truly believing that has gotten me through a lot. You know those times in life when you've heard something a million times before but for some reason this time it really spoke to you? This was one of those moments.

To be honest, I'm not sure where I got the next phrase I'm going to use, but it's very powerful if you'll let it become a part of your life. When the enemy tries to come in and remind you of your past, use this. This is the question: *What are you characterized by?*

Are you letting your past sin and pain dictate who you are and *whose* you are today? If so, knock it off and start a new you. Start being characterized by something different. If you're struggling with letting go, remind yourself that that was who you were—not who you are today. In the times that I feel as though I'm being chastised, I ask myself this question: Am I characterized by this? If so, I work diligently to correct that behavior. If not, then I mark it as a one-time thing and choose not to dwell on it. I choose to dwell on those things that give praise to God. Go ahead and read Philippians 4:8 right now. I'm not going to put it in here for you. I want you to be characterized by going to the Word of God and meditating on it.

Philippians 4:8 has become a life verse for me. The way I define a life verse is one that replays over and over in your mind and life—one that you want to be characterized by. When my youngest daughter, Lauren, was just a few years old, I received a call at work saying that my wife had found her floating in her cousin's swimming pool, lifeless and her eyes rolled into the back of her head. In what was one of the longest drives of my life, even though it was only fifteen minutes, I was overwhelmed and relieved when I arrived and saw Lauren in my wife's arms and reaching for me. In the aftermath of it all, my wife struggled with thoughts of being a bad mother and all the what ifs. While we were talking one day, she told me that God asked her to apply Philippians 4:8 to her life. She told God that there was nothing good in that situation, but he spoke very clearly to her that Lauren was living, and did *not* die. That scripture became a life verse to her that day, and it saved her from mental anguish. God gave her Philippians 4:8 to hold on to, and I've used it ever since.

You see, we had to find the praiseworthy things to meditate on. Sometimes that looks like every other second, and then there will be times when life is flowing smoothly and you won't need it as often.

I've said all of that to lead to my next point. I want to be characterized as a man who praises God through it all—not just the parts that I think I can handle, not just the times when everything is pleasant, and not just the times when I'm riding on cloud nine. I am praising him all the time—in it all and through it all.

I've been a worship pastor/leader for a little over six years now, and praising God is a deep-seated passion of mine. Praising comes naturally for me when it comes to leading God's people. It's not where the rubber meets the road though. Praising God is not limited to the congregational lifting of his name. In fact, that's an extremely small part of what praising is all about. Let's set some things in place so we can further establish where I'm heading.

Praise is not worship, and worship is not praise. I am talking completely and solely about praise in this chapter. Just like worship, praise is a lifestyle but held in a different context. Worship is an intimate encounter with God from a grateful heart declaring his worth. Praise is a celebration of his goodness with intentional expression.

> **Worship is an intimate encounter with God from a grateful heart declaring His worth. Praise is a celebration of His goodness with intentional expression.**

Praise is active, and it also activates the power of God's presence in your life. Praise sets you up for worship! Praise humbles you by taking the focus off of you and placing it on him. When you enter into his presence and begin to praise him, you cannot focus on you. And when you're unable to focus on you, true praise begins.

Praise is an attitude of the heart—not just a fast song sung on Sunday mornings. You see, when we truly understand that praise is meant to be woven into every part of our lives, in takes on new meaning. *When we develop an attitude of praise, we are not concerned with the why—we are focused on the worth.* Have you ever caught yourself asking, "What am I doing? Why?" When our hearts are completely satisfied and sold out to Jesus, the questions turns into, "Where and when, God?" Can you see the difference? Our entire Christian walk is about dying to ourselves to see

Jesus made alive through us. In the area of praise, we must die to what we think and live the way he deserves.

As it pertains to praise on Sunday mornings, this next part is for the men. It can apply to you as well, ladies, but it truly is more of a male issue, and it hacks me off.

If you're of the male type reading this right now, let me make something very clear. And the main reason I'm speaking to the men right now is because I see this as an epidemic stifling our country. Standing with your arms crossed during praise and worship on a Sunday morning is a sure fire way to let the worship pastor/leader, more importantly God, know that you're heart is not in the right place. The only person you're fooling with your macho image is yourself.

Just so you know what you're dealing with in me, I've successfully rifle-hunted elk in Colorado, antelope in Montana, and whitetail in Texas. I recently took up bow hunting, and I've been blessed to hunt whitetail in Minnesota as well as Texas, and I can't wait to go on a safari hunt in Africa. I love to shoot guns, ride motorcycles, and anything else that gets the blood pumping. I successfully completed the JFK fifty-mile run held in Maryland. I've served my country in the United States Air Force, was a police officer for three years outside of the military, and I've trained with the Army Rangers. So let's not kid each other with the line that you're a man's man and they don't do that. King David was a man's man and praised God unashamed.

I've heard all the excuses. "It's just my personality." "I don't need to prove anything." Yes, you do. There's a world out there that needs to see men unashamedly praise God in all of his glory. In most men's efforts to prove that they don't need to prove anything, they're proving how unwilling they are to fully submit to him. We need real men to fess up to the fact that it makes them uncomfortable. So how do we get to where it's not so uncomfortable? Just like anything else, practice and keep after it until it is! Here's the recurring theme again—*don't stop*! As I talked about this in the previous chapter, we have to get in tune with our motives for why we do what we do. Method is important, but motive trumps that. True praise comes through understanding that his desire overrides yours. King David, by most standards, was not a good husband, nor was he a good father to his children. But David *did* understand one thing that would sustain him as he walked out his life. He understood how to praise and place God first.

The Bible declares David was a man after God's own heart! Why? Because he knew how to praise. It certainly wasn't that David had an incredible amount of character. From a little boy, David trusted in the Lord and praised him through every circumstance. When David was down, he praised him; when he was high on life, he praised him; and when everything was peachy, he praised him. As it says in Psalms 34:1, "Of David, when he changed his behavior before Abimelech, so that he drove him out, and he went away. I will bless the LORD at all times; his praise shall continually be in my mouth" (Psalm 34:1, ESV).

David proclaimed that he would bless the Lord at *all* times and praise would continually be in his mouth. What a powerful declaration! Grasping this truth will turn your life around. When God can trust that you are going to praise him at all times, watch out, baby!

What if the turnaround you've been so desperately seeking for your life came down to this one principle? Praise. What if all that was holding you back was you? What would you have to lose if you chose to get alone with God and praise him even though you don't understand or see the bigger picture yet? Isn't that what faith is? Praising God even when we can't see? The reality is that you lose nothing and gain everything. It's as practical as getting alone and just opening up a conversation with God. Telling him that even though you can't see or even understand why everything that's happening to you is happening, you're still going to praise him.

I'm sure that you've never managed to extremely upset someone before, but I have. I once was hired for a job that other candidates should have received due to credentials, but the boss was looking for other qualities—qualities that I happened to possess. When I first started in this new position, I had several coworkers, who had also applied for my position, upset with me. Even though I was perplexed as to why they were mad at me and not the boss, I decided to apply this praising principle to the situation.

It for sure did not happen overnight. When one or both of them would give me the cold shoulder, I would just praise God for my job and that he was working on their hearts to soften them toward me. When I would get killer stares from across the room, I would praise God that he is greater in me than he who is in the world (1 John 4:4).

I will never forget the day I received an email from the coworker who treated me the worst. It was a forward of a joke he wanted me to see. I wasn't sure at first whether or not it was a good thing, but then he came to my office, eager to talk about the email. I was taken back at first, but then I knew that all the praising was paying off and I give God *all* the glory. I am still friends with him, and I truly enjoy our times together.

Here's what the Word of God says praise is in Hebrews 13:15 (esv), "Through Him let us continually offer up a sacrifice of praise to God, that is, the fruit of lips that acknowledge His name." This is an absolutely incredible verse and insight to what praise is—lips that praise his name all the time! No matter what, when, where, or why, we should be acknowledging how great God is. With lips that acknowledge his name, we will not only change our future but the future of the generations we are influencing. Whether you want to believe it or not, you're influencing people. You're doing this either by intentionally pouring into them or by doing nothing. The generation to come and the one that went before us are watching to see what we will do next. It's a great responsibility, and we need to get excited about fulfilling it. We need to praise God. We need to acknowledge his name.

But can I encourage you that it's not enough to just say it? You need to *live* it. When you praise, you develop and nurture a positive lifestyle. If you feel as though you're constantly negative about most things, try praising God to a positive outlook.

As I've learned to praise God through the darkest moments of my life, I've been overwhelmingly blessed by the depths and heights of where my relationship with Jesus has gone. I now know that I would have never experienced this without praising him through it all. When Jesus can trust that you will praise him through every circumstance and not just *some*, exciting things begin to take place.

So what does it look like? When you feel like giving up, praise him. When your boss is being a jerk for the umpteenth time, praise him. When you got the job you've been praying for, praise him. When you've been let go for any reason, praise him. When your girlfriend said yes to marrying you, praise him. When you've just had your heart broken by a friend or significant other, praise him. Are you getting it? No matter what this life throws our way, we must praise him! Don't believe that the lie that you praise him *for* the bad situations that happen. You praise him for being faithful *through* those times.

Praise positions you for the favor of the Lord. I don't believe that God owes us anything, but I *do* believe in the power of his Word. When we openly praise the Lord through every trial, pain, joy, love, circumstance, and situation, we unlock the potential for the Word of God to take over our lives! Let his praise be in your mouth at all times.

You have permission.

PERMISSION TO POSITION

I'd be lying to you if I said that as I spoke to my pastor that I wasn't wondering about whether or not I'd maintain my position as the worship pastor. The things that haunted me from years ago were keeping me from the future things God had in store. God wasn't holding those things back from me—I was! I was allowing the current position of my mind to defeat me before I even got started.

I have to admit that even today as I move forward in the things of God, I have to renew the position of my mind to the Lord's. As you have no doubt concluded by now, all of the chapters in this book intertwine, and we grow in them as we lay our lives down at his feet.

Obviously, by the grace of God I was able to maintain my position at our church. Now let me pose a question. Who do you think is going to be more loyal and faithful to God and the ministry they're serving under?

1. The person who just believes that God is for him.

2. The person who has intimate knowledge of and has experienced that God is for him.

If you answered number one, please seek immediate medical attention. If you answered number two, then you're right. It's obvious, isn't it? So here's my encouragement to all the leaders out there right now with someone under them going through some junk. Show them that not only God believes in them, but you do too. That is not to say that there are not consequences for our actions. Believe me, there were plenty of consequences I've had to face. There's a huge difference in facing those consequences alone and actually having someone there to walk beside you.

Without a doubt, my wife has been my biggest supporter and encourager. She has believed in me through it all, and I am inexpressibly in debt to her. She is dedicated to growing into the woman of God she is called to be. I've never met a person more devoted to maturing in the things of Christ. She constantly sharpens me in the Word of God. What a gift I have in her!

To all the women, it is completely true that you can come alongside your man and help him become a better one. I'm living proof of being a screw up and watching the love of Christ displayed through my wife. It's not an easy road, but it's more than worth it. You owe it to Christ, yourself, your husband, and kids to live this principle out. You will never regret doing what's right in the eyes of our Savior. Here's what I've learned about positioning yourself for success.

From my experience, pain and position go hand in hand. Here's why I believe this. There's no possible way for you to die to yourself without pain. It's impossible! Death equals pain, and pain equals death. In some way, this always rings true. To what degree, level, or type of pain is what I *can't* tell you. Again, this is why I believe most people give up. When you press through the pain, you begin to see the position of where God is taking you. But you never see that position without the pain. If Jesus wasn't exempt from this, why should we think that *we* are?

Some of us see the position that God wants to take us, and it freaks us out! We are overwhelmed by the calling, and it causes us to abandon the mission altogether. The worst thing we can do is become calloused to our calling. Numb from the cost of what the calling will take, we sabotage our success before we ever take one step in its direction.

Please understand that I'm not saying that Jesus causes your pain. What I am saying is that we are not exempt from pain in this world. In fact, God uses the pain to show us things if we will let him. I've witnessed many people go through pain only to come out on the other side no better off—sometimes worse. Why in the world would we go through pain and not choose to learn lessons along the way.

This is where relationships and accountability come in handy. You need people in your life that recognize the pain you're going through and make sure you get positioned for success.

If anything I've learned over the last few years of working for our church full time, it's that relationships are the foundation of everything God has for you. But you have to position yourself for the right relationships. God built everything on the premise that we would surround ourselves with relationships. He positioned Adam in a place that offered close relationship to him. Then he said that it wasn't good for Adam to be alone—again, relationship. Some of you are only a relationship away from your destiny and/or dreams.

Some of you are only a relationship away from your destiny and/or dreams.

For some that may mean giving one up, and for others it could mean taking one on. First and foremost, you must position yourself in His presence to have relationship with Him.

I've heard that the definition of insanity is doing the same thing over and over again while expecting different results. If you don't want to be where you are now, you are going to have to change the position of where you've been. This may involve changing jobs, but from my experience, that's the exception and not the rule. In most cases, this requires us to reposition our minds to think in a new way.

I can't think like I did in my twenties, thirties, or forties and expect my thirties, forties, and fifties to be different or better. In other words, we need to grow up. Here's what the Word of God says about the way we think. Romans 12:2 says, "Do not be conformed to this world, but be transformed by the renewal of your mind, that by testing you may discern what is the will of God, what is good and acceptable and perfect."

Here's a great way of looking at this verse. Don't position yourself to be *con*-formed, in other words, conned into a fake, false, and futile way of doing things. Position yourself to be *trans*-formed, to go across, to change thoroughly, and go beyond just any old form.

A couple of years back, my wife and I were privileged to go through a course that radically changed our lives. It was called "The Pacific Institute." This program is designed around changing the way that you think. My wife and I were amazed at some of the ways we were thinking that were completely unproductive, even sabotaging. I highly recommend attending one of these seminars and investing in your life. We were negative and didn't even realize we had self-defeating thoughts. In a lot of ways, we felt conned by our own minds, but we weren't staying there, and neither are *you* going to anymore.

All of us, at one time or another, have been conned, whether by bringing it on ourselves or by an unfortunate circumstance in which people have taken advantage of us.

It's often much more painful and harder to get over when we've done it to ourselves. If someone else has hurt us, we have a source to blame and can remove that source from our lives. When it's us, we still have to wake up to that person and hear that "head voice" beat us up over and over again. That's why it's so important to follow what the Word of God declares. The Word helps us to stop focusing on the fake, false, and futile way of doing things. It helps us to start changing our mindset and believe the truth over our lives—much easier read than done, I know, but it's possible.

Yeah, everyone has been conned, but not everyone has been transformed. Transformation allows you to take on a whole new life. You're not staying in the old way of doing things; you're moving on, changing, and going beyond what you once thought was possible. You're positioning yourself to be used in a far greater capacity. When people begin the transformation process, their walk with God increases at an exponential rate. The Word of God tells us in Ephesians 3:20 (NIV), "to Him who is able to do immeasurably more than all we ask or imagine, according to His power that is at work in us." It's through Him, that we can do more!"

I will admit that at times it's difficult to not dwell on the regrets of the former mistakes I've made, but you and I can't afford to stay there.

I am loyal to the core—so much so that at times I can be more loyal to the place I am in life rather than getting out of my comfort zone and into what God has called me to.

It's so much easier to get in a place that's familiar and not rock the boat—to bask in a life that doesn't have much risk and offers little, to no reward. But we're really not sure the reward is worth it, so we stay and never position ourselves to do greater things. We even use such phrases like, "Oh, I'm just waiting on God and listening to find out what's next." What we're really saying is that we're freaked out by what's around the corner and where I am right now feels pretty good, even though it's not great!

If most of us were honest, we'd like to have no risk and high reward, but that's not the way it works. And to consistently overcome, we must get out of our comfort zone and go after those rewards.

Maybe you can relate to this. I love all kind of sports, and as a kid I had a real love of baseball. I was a pitcher and wasn't too bad either. I pitched for years, and then it all changed with one meeting. I got the opportunity to meet a professional pitcher, Stan Klick of the 1956 Detroit Tigers. I was blessed enough to spend an afternoon with him as he gave me some pointers. Here's the key. He taught me how to position the ball for the greatest delivery. Now, at this point I could have been young and naïve and said, "What does this old man know? I'm doing fine on my own." I was still young and naïve, but I took his advice, and my pitching accuracy increased significantly.

I applied his method, even though it took some getting used to. It was difficult to adapt to his strategy, especially when I was getting along fine with my own. But I wanted to do it the best way—not just a good way. Through the meeting, I was able to pitch a no-hitter in an All-Star game. I was able to do much greater with the wisdom of one who went before me and was much better than I.

So often though, this is what we do. Someone who has been there and knows a little more, maybe even a lot more, offers to position us to deliver a better us to this world, and we get pious or even offended. One of the greatest frustrations is being a person who can see the path that someone is heading down leads to destruction and the person won't listen. I've had many people in my office who've come seeking counsel only to reject what's offered. I'm in no way saying that I know it all, but I do my very best to point people to the Word of God. I watched them spiral downward all the while my heart is breaking for them. If that's not enough, I've even been blamed as the reason for their decline. Again my heart breaks for them. This is where we have to put our pride down and allow God to use others to position us. We get conned into living the same old life year after year and never truly grow and mature the way we're supposed to because we're not positioning ourselves to be transformed into his image.

Positioning doesn't always look pretty either. Consider Joseph, for example. His positioning led him into a pit, slavery, false accusations, prison, and finally to his destiny—the palace! I'm sure Joseph had some questions and concerns along the way, but he never gave up hope that where he was positioned at the moment would lead him to his destination. Where are you today that you may be discouraged by your position? Would you take a moment a put into practice what you've all ready learned or have been refreshed by?

1. *Proclaim* the Word of God over your situation right now.

2. *Pray* that God would encourage your heart.

3. *Praise* him for all that he's done, doing, and going to do.

4. Now you're starting to get into *position* to make a real difference.

Just taking a couple of minutes to put these principles into practice makes all the difference. It's truly amazing when we utilize the Word of God what he does in and through us. Seriously, though, don't move on until you've taken three to five minutes (more if you'd like) to apply this right now.

I want to give you just a couple more practical ways to position yourself for success. Start paying attention to your body. Are you tired or fully awake? We know we need to get into the Word of God, but we try doing it when we're beat or overly tired. Don't get stuck in the mindset that you have to read eighteen chapters of the Bible every time you sit down to read. Find a time when you're fully awake and alert and tackle five verses and meditate on them. Ask questions and research them. This will position you to retain what you're reading and not to feel defeated for not reading more.

God designed our bodies to talk to us and let us know what's going on. We need to pay attention to what they're telling us. You've got too much to accomplish for the kingdom of God to not do this.

Early in my marriage, my wife and I struggled so much that most days, we were just roommates. Those days turned into several years. During this time all I wanted to do was get away and forget about all my problems. I definitely checked out of my relationship with Tisa and my responsibilities as a father. I started looking for thrills, really just looking for anything to make me feel alive again. I was trying to play all the pain away and it wasn't working. For a moment playing feels good and does make you forget, but there is never any long-term sense of satisfaction or peace.

I had to start believing that God had a purpose for me again—that the pain would actually be used for something and that it wouldn't just be pain. Maybe you're trying to play all the pain away, or maybe you're on an extended pause in your life and you know God is drawing you out of it. Stop resisting today because I assure you that he has an incredible plan for you.

Another step you can take is to find your favorite scriptures and put them on post-it notes all throughout your house as a reminder and encouragement every time you see them. I love what my sister-in-law has done in her bathroom. She took lipstick and wrote down several verses on her mirror. It may seem simple, but it's extremely effective. Position the Word of God to overtake you and lead you into a relationship with Him that rocks your world. Don't underestimate the power of what this will do in your life.

Now go on and give yourself permission to position.

PERMISSION TO PLAY/PAUSE

There will be seasons in our lives that are crazier than others, but there has to be a balance achieved in all of this. Here's why. People can get so consumed with the work of the ministry that they begin to feel as though God will never be able to do what he needs to do without them.

For all of you who just freaked out over that statement, you're exactly who I'm talking to. Yes, God uses us to accomplish his will on the earth, but too many become borderline pious in the way they handle ministry. God wants to use you, is using you, and will continue to use you, but I believe it's dangerous when we truly believe it can't be done without *me*. This is a prideful stance, and we all know where pride leads.

This is why I believe playing/pausing is such an important part of the Christian walk because too many Christians need to go to the doctor and have the stick surgically removed. You get around some Christians and feel bad for smiling or laughing. This is crazy! Please understand that I take my walk with God extremely seriously and never make light of his outrageous sacrifice. But he is also the author of humor and fun. In him all things are made and are for our benefit. We need to learn how to play and laugh a little more.

Jesse Duplantis is a well-known minister, and he tells the story of time when he was first in the ministry and was staying in the home of a local minister. He woke up to see a black figure in the corner of the room. He began to pray against the enemy only to discover quite some time later, after he turned on the lights, that it was a coat on a coat rack! I personally believe that God was laughing like crazy over that one! I can just imagine God trying to tell Jesse that it wasn't an evil force or demon and then just belly laughing because he knew Jesse would turn on the lights and realize what was really going on.

Have you ever tripped going up the stairs and praised God that no one was around to see you? I've got news for you. God saw it, and he probably laughed—only, of course, if you weren't hurt…badly. I've got in the habit of talking to God when I find myself in situations like these. For example, if I just got finished tripping on stairs, my conversation with God would go something like this, "Did you see that, God? Please don't tell anyone in a vision."

I often tell my children that a key to success in this life is to learn to laugh at yourself. You need to learn the art of laughing at yourself.

> ## You need to learn the art of laughing at yourself.
> · · · · · · · · · · · · · · ·

Join in the laughter of others at you or with you. It's funny, and you should never be caught depriving someone of a good belly laugh.

I believe we take the Word of God seriously and our walk with him, but we can't take ourselves too seriously. When we do, we miss out. Our goal is to lead people to Jesus and make disciples. Nobody wants to be the disciple of a stick in the mud. Seek to explore every part and characteristic of our King, not just the ones that fit into your little box of who he is. Playing/pausing is essential when it comes to having gone through a tough season in life. We all know that we go through ups and downs. Sometimes, those downs are weeks, months, or even years. We've got to let off some steam, get refreshed, and be ready to serve God at full capacity.

I certainly don't believe that it's just the work of serving Jesus that get's people burned out. It may be that you're consumed by chasing toddlers around, running from one sporting event to another for your children, getting over-involved in church, community clubs, etc. I caution you to insist on running your life and not letting your life run you. In one of the dark moments of my life, I had to learn to "let it go and let God." I had to take a step back and realize that a drained leader/person has nothing to give. Or if they do give, it's watered down by their own insufficiencies. The Bible says God is *all* sufficient; we are just *some* sufficient. We have to take moments to rest, relax, and get refilled.

I didn't necessarily take a break from my duties, but I *did* schedule in some down time and even some fun time. Now, what I have come to hear from others who have been very transparent is that during their down time they don't read the Word or get into his presence. This is not good. There's not a day that should go by without us talking and conversing with God. We not only need it, but it's a biblical mandate.

For clarification purposes, I want to attempt to define what playing/pausing is and is not. As I just stated, playing/pausing is a time of refreshment and rejuvenation. It may consist of taking a three-day weekend and getting away with your family or by yourself. You may decide to go hiking, camping, fishing, hunting, or just go to the lake. Maybe you just make some sandwiches, go to a local park, and have a picnic once a week. Whatever it is, it needs to be something that takes your mind off of everything else but the moment at hand. You need to expose yourself to experiencing some down time. You'll be surprised at how much your attitude will be transformed by this simple act. On the flip side, too much down town time will create an apathetic attitude toward life. Again, there is certainly a balance in all of it.

Playing/pausing is not doing whatever you want whenever. I've met quite a few of these people. They believe that life is all about playing. Too much of this can really hurt your witness for Jesus. People in the end will not take these people seriously, and the reality is that these people are focused on one thing—and it's not Jesus. When all you live for is the next thrill or adventure, you're chasing after a feeling and not a relationship with God. Relationships are incredibly exciting at times and mundane at others. They are not always about what feels good at the moment, and this is why it's dangerous to live for the moment all the time.

Understanding that you weren't placed in this world just for you is of paramount importance. Jesus understood that his life was not to be lived by his own desires or will. That thrill you seek will only lead to emptiness and the sense of a life void of meaning.

I know that it may sound as if I'm contradicting myself by saying take some "me" time… wait it's not about you. Both are true, and that's where balance takes its role.

We can't play/pause all the time because we have a mandate from God. But when we neglect to ever play/pause, we burn out and are worse off than when we started. Take a moment to think about what playing/pausing looks like to you. What activities or lack thereof do you need to take place in your life? How long will this be? What do you hope to get out of it?

Asking yourself these questions will give you a starting place.

Playing permitted.

PERMISSION TO PRACTICE

This is where it all comes together. You can know all of these things, but if you don't put them into practice, they are like a hammer and nail never picked up. You have to pick up the hammer and strategically place the nail and put some action behind it for its full potential. So it goes with all the previous chapters. You have to put these principles to work in your life. And just because you practice doesn't mean you're going to get it right all the time. But you can bet your fanny that if you don't practice, you will for sure get it wrong.

I lead a band practice several times a week, and there are some songs that we have played and sung over a million times it seems, but we still practice…why? Because even though it's familiar, we don't want to allow apathy to creep in and rob what God wants to do. I've had people come in who are completely unprepared to sing or play because they have not practiced. This is very annoying, and you come to not expect much from these people. The same thing happens when it comes to real life, so we need to take this same approach to our daily lives. Let's not give in to laziness and never fully explore the potential God has placed into each one of us. Hebrew 5:14 (NASB) says, "But solid food is for the mature, who because of practice have their senses trained to discern good and evil."

The more we put into practice these principles, the more we will be entrusted with eating the solid food of the Word. I don't know about you, but if you lay a steak down in front of me or a glass of milk, I may cut you to get to the steak. When we don't practice we are essentially saying, "Give me the glass of milk." The Word of God is rich and able to sustain. Let's eat the meat!

Practicing shakes off the rust and keeps us sharp. It keeps us focused on what is truly important and sheds away all the unnecessary things that take up too much of our time. So would you join me in following these six simple steps to living a successful life devoted to Jesus?

1. *Proclaim* the Word of God

2. *Pray* for a real relationship with Him

3. *Praise* Him at all times

4. *Position* yourself for greatness

5. *Play/Pause* and have fun

6. *Practice* and repeat

My practicing over the years has not looked so graceful at times. I've battled trying to remember, "Why do I believe these things?" Or thinking, *This is getting me nowhere at the moment.* And I will be brutally honest by saying I've come back to this book for reminders at times. When my wife and I are contenders in intense moments of fellowship (arguing), it has not always been at the forefront of my mind to put these principles into practice. But therein lies my point. As long as we're on this side of eternal life with Jesus we will have to practice and you can be sure that we'll have plenty of opportunities.

One of my friends, Keil, once told me after hearing me quote the phrase "practice makes perfect" that I was wrong. With much joy, I ignored his delusions of being right until he persisted. He said, "*Perfect* practice makes perfect."

Perfect practice make perfect.
· ·

To be completely honest, at first, I really didn't get it. But to my defense, I was in my twenties, and who really knows anything in their twenties? But then it hit me that he was right.

We can spend our whole lives practicing something that is nowhere close to perfect. People make the choice all the time to live (practice) life without much thought or purpose behind their actions. We trek along practicing a system that to say is flawed would be a gross understatement. All the while we get frustrated, defeated, and demoralized because something in us desires what seems unreachable, or at least unobtainable. Trusting in our own devices, we lead ourselves into a cycle of chaos.

But we must break this cycle and realize that there is a perfect system out there, and the more we practice that perfect system, the more we are being perfected!

If you by chance are wondering where this perfect system exists, well look no further than the Word of God (Matthew 5:48, Ephesians 5:1).

When we jump off the diving board with everything we've got into His Word, we are then called to become perfect as he is perfect (Matthew 5:48). The act of perfectifying (not a true English word, but you have to admit that you're gonna start using that one) becomes our lifestyle and motive. And when our motive lines up with what the Word of God says, then we begin to see transformation take place.

It is my complete honor that you've read this book, and I pray that your life is truly transformed by these principles. This life may not be easy, but following these steps is not impossible, either.

As I have lived these steps out, I have seen the favor of God rest over me and my family. Again, I pray that your life is transformed by the Word of God and the life of Jesus. Remember, it's not merely about the method—it's mainly about the motive. Just don't stop; whatever you do, don't stop!